My Ukr

Edited by Dr Julie-Anne Sykley

Publisher: Julie-Anne Sykley, Darwin, Australia
via Amazon Kindle Direct Publishing
First Published: 2017
Text copyright Julie-Anne Sykley (Editor) © 2018
Cover design Jasmynie Voznyk

About the Editor

Dr Julie-Anne Sykley is an Australian psychologist with 30 years professional experience helping people. She is of Ukrainian background and her first language is Ukrainian.

Acknowledgements

I am sincerely grateful for the support of...
Professor Marko Pavlyshyn (Ukrainian Studies, Monash University, Melbourne) – for expertly guiding the presentation of this book. Iryna Stepanova – for typing all the children's comments in Ukrainian. Kateryna Lytvyn and Maria Veres – for translating the children's comments so competently from Ukrainian into English. Dmytro Stepanova – for translating selected excerpts. Yuri Tkacz (Bayda Books) – for professional guidance.

The Directors Zinchyk Volodymyr Volodymyrovych, Savchyk Viktor Mykolayovych, and Ctadnik Ruslan Anatoliyvych, and staff, at: Zahalnoosvitnaya Shkola I-III Stupenya-Himnaziya; Zahalnoosvitnaya Shkola I-III No.1; and Shkola Holoniv (Volyn, Ukraine).

A *huge* thank you from my heart to every *child* and *family* involved with this book. You're brilliant!

Contents

Foreword

Ukraine has an ancient history, a rich culture, and striking natural beauty. Since the collapse of the Soviet Union and Russia's invasion after the Maidan, the effect on Ukraine has been devastating. In the last 100 years alone, Ukraine has suffered two World Wars, Soviet tyranny, a nuclear catastrophe, and a premeditated Famine that murdered several million people.

Present-day Ukraine is at war with Russia, which is "the direct result of Russian President Vladimir Putin's efforts to establish control over Ukraine" (Atlantic Council, May 2015, preface). Corruption is prevalent in politics and all levels of government. Widespread poverty and alcohol abuse thrives. Trapped in this terrible crisis: the children of Ukraine.

When I travelled to Ukraine April to June 2016, I visited schools in West Ukraine to talk to students and offer words of encouragement to young people (East Ukraine is currently at war, so it was too dangerous to travel there). The children were keen to share their views, so I suggested producing a "book" of thoughts as a way to empower them. The students were delighted with the idea of telling their stories to the world.

I asked the children to write down what Ukraine means to them, what kinds of things worried them, and how they envisaged the future. The result? A collection of stirring reflections highlighting Ukraine's natural beauty, devotion to country, anguish about war, and a desire to be free.

Not only is this book a snapshot of thoughts from Ukrainians aged seven to seventeen years, it is an exclusive glimpse inside the *soul* of Ukraine's youth. But this book is no children's story. It is an account of experiences, as told by children for everyone, especially adults. It is a chorus of innocent hearts striving to tackle adversity by singing in a little book, and reaching out to the world for support... and love.

To help you hear, and feel, each child's message yourself, I have reproduced the children's thoughts as accurately as possible. I have not interpreted or paraphrased the comments. This truly makes it *their* story. As you read their stories, you will surely adore many young Ukrainians. Deep in their hearts, the children of Ukraine hope that people around the world hear them. Is anyone out there listening?

Dr Julie-Anne Sykley BBsc *(Hons) MAPS PhD*
Psychologist

What is Ukraine to you?

A Beautiful Place...

– Marianna Leyskiv, 8 years

For us in Volyn flowers are blooming,
Their magic seems to charm everyone.

Come to Volyn and your soul will sing,
And people will run to you with warm
welcomes.

Our Volyn – this is a fairytale natural
environment.

Mountains, fields, forests, and
gardens.

– Anna Kas'ko, 12 years

Ukraine for me – is the blossoming of guelder rose beside every house. It is the tinkling song of the nightingales and larks, the magical notes of a mother's lullaby, the crying of storks and the clear light of morning. This is a land, where you want to come back to again and again...
– Sofia Stepaniuk, 11 years

I love my Ukraine for its yellow and fertile fields of wheat and the blue sky. My family is here, my relatives, my friends, and everything dearest in my life.
– Yulia Oshurkevych, 11 years

Ukraine means for me: wide steppes, deep lakes, and flowering fields. In the future I see my country as peaceful and flourishing.
– Valentyn Sheshko, 11 years

I love my Ukraine for its beauty of nature, kindness.
— Diana Mikulska, 9 years

I love my country for its beauty, for its harmonious language, for its unchanging traditions.
— Kateryna Hensetska, 14 years

I love my colourful Ukraine for its quiet waters and bright stars, green gardens, white houses, fields of golden wheat, for its blue boundless sky...
— Alexandra Konopatska, 16years

I love Ukraine because she has natural beauty, mountains, seas.
– Maxym Yarema, 8 years

Ukraine is very beautiful. It has got marvellous forests, fields, lakes and rivers.
– Daria Kamatska, 8 years

Oh you, mum – Ukraine,
I love you,
Black sea, wide steppes, green Carpathians
Beneath a dark blue sky
The path home.
– Anna Vitriv, 13 years

I love Ukraine because of its natural beauty. And there are also a lot of rivers, lakes, and forests. The most friendly people live in Ukraine.
— Myroslava Kondratyuk, 9 years

I am a citizen of Ukraine and I love my country for the blue skies, yellow fields, lush seas, and high mountains.
— Sofiya Davydyuk, 12 years

My native land, and my town is beautiful. I love it for its steppes, mountains, and forests.
— Diana Mikulska, 9 years

— Roman Veres, 4 years

I love you Ukraine, my dear country!
I love the low rustle of your groves!
I love your golden, fragrant fields,
Dear to me are the Dnipro and the
cliffs!
The cherry tree garden next to our
house,
The Ukrainian edge to our rich songs.

— Ulyana Kolesnik, 12 years

Ukraine is... the cloudless sky and boundless golden fields of wheat. I love her for her beautiful views of lakes and rivers, forests, valleys and snowy mountain peaks. And because kind people live here, who care about making morals and the spirit strong.
– Andrij Kulish, 11 years

Ukraine – its ancient history, vast fields, the Carpathians, and Crimea. We are proud of its scenic landscapes. Ukrainians are friendly and versatile people, with a sincere soul and faith in God. Ukraine is a melodic and magical nation.
– Anna Vitriv, 13 years

Ukraine for me – is the beauty of nature, people's kindness, earth's generosity.
– Valeria Pyroh, 8 years

I love my Ukraine for her forests, flowering gardens, and pleasant language like the song of the blue-tit.
— Anna Prysyazna, 13 years

Ukraine is my birthplace. It is the dearest place on earth, my native land. Here there are forests, mountains, steppes, meadows, rivers, and lakes. The beauty of my Motherland is – unmeasurable. I love Ukraine.
— Sophia Yuzvyk, 12 years

Ukraine is one with us, like a mother. Her eyes are blue – they are the indigo lakes and blue waves of the rivers.
— Alina Muzychuk, 15 years

Ukraine... She is in everything that surrounds us: in the moon, in the stars, in the path we take to go to school, in every stone and tree. She is everything that is native and dear to each of us. And the red guelder rose, which grows on the ground near our home, and the towel embroidered with grandmother's old hands. Ukraine – this is our native land, our home, our country. With a glorious centuries-old history and wise, talented people, rich folk traditions, striking scenery, with a magical song, that charms the whole world.
– Diana Moroz, 13 years

I really love my country, because I was born here, grew up and live here. This scenic country calls us with its beauty, our green groves, meadows are the most beautiful in the world.
– Yuriy Dyadyuk, 12 years

How can one not love my yellow-blue country? I love her fields, forests and mountains, the full rivers and lakes, the melodious language of nightingales, folk customs and traditions. I love her because Taras H. Shevchenko and our Volynian Leysa Ukrainka loved her.
– Olga Zhuk, 15 years

For me, Ukraine – is my birthplace. This is my native land, of flourishing green forests and boundless steppes. Ukraine for me, is like a mother, who protects me, who loves me and will never abuse! Ukraine – this is my life!
– Anastasia Vasilyuk, 12 years

Ukraine is a real miracle. Could you find another place on a planet, where endless steppes are gathered, where there are so many wonderful echoes and songs of birds? I love Ukraine sincerely, with all my heart!
— Alina Muzychuk, 15 years

My Ukraine, Ukraine,
Yellow wheat and blue sky.
How can I not love you, my dear one?
My heart hurts for your fate.
I want you to be free and strong,
For your enemies to die forever,
So that peace and harmony rule
On my land forever!
— Olga Zhuk, 15 years

Why do I love Ukraine? Gardens, fields, ponds. And more –a blue-blue sky and yellow fields of wheat
— Denys Horban, 12 years

Ukraine – is a gorgeous, blossoming earth. For me it is rivers, plains and mountains, the bright sun and heavenly blue, this is the language of my nightingale, this is the song that echoes in the heart.
— Mariya Krukovskaya, 13 years

Ukraine is rich in boundless steppes, thick forests, and deep lakes.
— Sofiya Davydyuk, 12 years

Ukraine – this is my homeland. It is fields, sown with strips of wheat and an endless sky. This is the Carpathian and Crimean mountains with their old trees and rivers. This is the broad Dnipro and the Black Sea.
– Anna Hayduk, 15 years

My Motherland – is cherries blossoming.
And willows over a pond, and guelder rose.
My Motherland – is harmony and peace.
And a bottomless, beautiful sky.
It is a magic song that echoes to the stars.
– Alina Muzychuk, 15 years

We are happy, that we were born and live in such a wonderful scenic land – in our beautiful Ukraine. How can you not love our songs, the melody of autumn forests, the winter blizzard, spring songs and the honeyed aromas of summer.
– Anna Kas'ko, 12 years

We have polluted the environment, we do not cherish nature. I don't want my country to become some great computer. I want to live like our grandfathers-ancestors. The main thing – it is up to people to behave decently and fairly.
– Vladislava Bohun, 14 years

– Nadiya Lakoma, 14 years

Ukraine – is my back up and support in any situation. Our scenic landscapes really help me.

In various life difficulties, you can simply watch nature and all your worries fly out somewhere far away into oblivion.

– Yuliya Petrushko, 15 years

A Country I Admire...

– Voronika Shyshko, 7 years

I love Ukraine, because – this is my land, I was born here and will grow up here to the end.

– Vadym Shtyn, 14 years

*I love my Ukraine because it is my Motherland.
Ukraine is my native land. I was born here, grew
up and go to school here. My family lives here. I
like our Ukrainian songs.*
– Alla Zvarko, 8 years

I love Ukraine, because it is my birthplace.
– Mukhail Rezhanovskey, 11 years

*Ukraine – is my birthplace.
This is my native country, native land.*
– Yulia Vavrenyuk, 14 years

I love my Ukraine because it is my Motherland.
Our Ukraine has good, hard-working people.
– Daria Kamatska, 8 years

Why do I love Ukraine? Because I am Ukrainian!
Because I was born here, in my village, my
parents, a brother.
– Denis Horban, 12 years

Every step, every corner, is dear to me. And that
willow tree that leans over the water's edge, and
the little well at the edge of the road – all this
inspires joyful memories.
– Alina Lashchuk , 12 years

I love my Ukraine because, I was born here, I live and study here. My parents, my grandfather and grandmother, parents and all my ancestors were born here. I love my country because it has the richest nature, and the most fertile soil. I love her because hardworking people live here, and I love our Ukrainian language, because it is the sweetest in the world.
– Roman Kondratyuk, 12 years

I love Ukraine for her independence. For her bravery, strength, courage, beauty. My Ukraine is everything for me.
– Vadum Nychyporuk, 13 years

I love my Ukraine because my roots are here, because I was born here and live here.
– Victoria Trach, 13 years

I love Ukraine! How can you not love a homeland for its immense rivers, fields, for her songs, customs, and traditions?
– Sophiya Yuzeffko, 14 years

Ukraine – this is my Motherland. She is as dear to me as my mother and father, as my family. I am proud to be Ukrainian. And I am proud that my country is the best in the world.
– Valeria Laschuk, 8 years

I love my country because it's my birthplace. Ukraine – she is my native home, which radiates her beauty and warmth. I believe, that everyone should love their country not for something, but that, she exists for you. Everything here is all yours – natively. I admire her Volynian forests, Carpathian mountains. People believe that it is better abroad – but this is not true!
– Alexandra Feoktysova, 12 years

– Daryna Fedchyk, 13 years

Ukraine – this is something more...
That which lives in my soul,
awakens the patriot in me, and
produces a mindful Ukrainian.

– Alexandra Konopatska, 16 years

Last year I was in Germany. It is nice, clean, very neat there. But there it is a foreign language, foreign traditions, other rules of life, which made me grieve for Ukraine.
– Daruna Stepanyuk, 12 years

I love Ukraine, because our people are very talented and hard-working. There are lovely and good people here, and wonderful and beautiful places in our country.
– Daria Ripolovs'ka, 14 years

Ukraine – this is a nation of decent people. I love her for her natural beauty, the melodic language of her songs. This is a home, to which I will always return.
– Olga Kas'ko, 14 years

I love my nation of Ukraine, first of all, because she is the only one for me, because, I was born and grew up here, and my parents live here.
I love our unsubdued people, our melodic language, our unsurpassed natural environment.
I love everything Ukrainian: from the West to the East, from the North to the South.
– Diana Moroz, 13 years

Ukraine, I love you! Warmth and soul – this is Ukraine! Everyone here is sincere and kind-hearted.
– Natalia Hrebenyuk, 13 years

Ukraine is and always will be in my heart, this is the beginning of my existence and the meaning in my life.
– Iryna Dubets, 15 years

Why do I love Ukraine? I was born here, live here and I thank God, that I was able to see the world.
– Yuliya Shchebetyuk, 15 years

They can't take a Motherland. The fragrant forests and fields, the fertile earth, the blue-eyed lakes, the singing nightingales, mother's lullabies – my Ukraine, never will I trade her for something else that is foreign.
– Serhii Tsekhosh, 12 years

Wherever I go, I will never forget my land!
– Yuriy Dyadyuk, 12 years

Ukraine – this is my future, this is my native land, the nightingale-like Ukrainian language. It is a rich cultural heritage, an embroidered shirt, and a vinok (hair-wreath) of cornflowers and poppies.
– Yuliya Loza, 12 years

Ukraine – is a pearl, she is unique! For me, Ukraine is – a dear land, hard-working people, folk traditions, fertile earth, and a second mother.
– Mariya Tsopko, 13 years

— Kateryna Matysevych, 11 years

*I love Ukraine because her
language is like the nightingales,
for the fact that, she has beautiful
fields. In Ukraine are the prettiest
girls and very good people.
Ukraine – is the best!
Glory to Ukraine!*

– Diana Holdovans'ka, 13 years

Ukraine for me is — hospitable, sincere, smiling people, a wonderful natural environment, and a musical language. Ukraine — this is a love deep in my heart. My native home is here, and people dear to my heart.
— Inna Kurda, 16 years

I'm sure, that for a true Ukrainian there can be no land better, than one' own native land.
— Yana Kurda, 14 years

"No one will build a nation for us, when we ourselves do not build it" (V. Lipinski).
— A quote about Ukraine contributed by Maria Tsopko, 13 years

Ukraine – this is my INDEPENDENT land! I was born here, and here I experienced joys and sorrows, here – is my home. My Ukraine – my soul!
Ukrainian, generous, joyful soul.
My Ukraine is – fertile land, friendly and hard-working people, deep lakes, fragrant flowers.
Just as a person can't be without a soul, then so am I without my mother Ukraine.
– Vladislav Bohun, 14 years

You must love your nation. Be a patriot of your country. Develop Ukrainian culture. Work for the well-being of your country. Protect nature and natural resources.
– Dariya Kamatska, 8 years

I am – Ukrainian. I didn't defend my country at war, and do not know enough about her history to sincerely writer about her. Ukraine, which I truly love, looks straightforward.

For the most part – this is my yard, my city, this is my family, the gardens and parks, which I love to visit, friends to whom I go to as a guest, grandmother's cottage in the village, and familiar animals.

Ukraine – is my Motherland. Today, adults and children feel the need to identify themselves as Ukrainians, to declare affection towards a glorious nation, with deep, thousand-year old roots. That is why we wear embroidered clothes often.

– Manuela Mindyuk, 13 years

What is Ukraine? For me – this is my birthplace, parents, black soil. It is the eternal song of nightingales, the song of mother's dear, warm lullaby. Ukraine – this is a little piece of me and my heart.
– Yana Kurda, 14 years

I love Ukraine for her fertile land, vast fields, red racemes of guelder rose and friendly, sincere people. I never want to leave this wonderful and dear country to me.
– Yuliya Petrushko, 15 years

– Veronika Severina, 12 years

I want to express my attitude towards Ukraine with Volodymyr Sosyuru's poem "Love Ukraine", famous around the world. An excerpt from the poem:

"Love Ukraine, like you love the sun,
Like the wind, and grass, and water,
In her happy hour and joyful flicker
Love her in the hour of the storm!...
Without her — we are nothing,
Like dust and smoke,
Scattered in the fields by the winds."

– Alexandra Konopatska, 16 years

What are your biggest
fears or worries?

The Present War...

— Viktoriya Bodnar

When strangers come...
They come to your home,
They kill you all and say:
"We're not guilty, not guilty".
Where is your mind?
Humanity cries.
You think you are gods
But everyone dies.
Don't choke my soul.
Our souls.

An excerpt from Jamala's Ukrainian song "1944", winner of the 2016 Eurovision Song Contest.

– Contributed by
Victoria Datsyuk, 7 years

I am very disappointed with these events, which take place in Ukraine. I have a very sore soul. It's when our men, parents, brothers go to war. When innocent people suffer. But we Ukrainians are strong, and we must protect our independent country from the enemy.
– Victoria Datsyuk, 7 years

I want the war in East Ukraine to end. People should be able to live in peace and happiness. Let all the nations of the world live as one family.
– Dariya Kamatska, 8 years

My heart feels terror.
– Maxym Yarema, 8 years

*My soul takes it hard when I look at the news.
Every time there are more and more wounded.
Ukraine loses its daughters and sons every day.*
– Yuliya Harbarchuk, 11 years

*A very high price is paid – human lives, and this
is very terrifying. My heart bleeds whenever I
remember events at the Maidan, when look at
the news in Donbas. My most cherished dream –
for war to finish as quickly as possible and let
peace come to our land.*
– Sophia Stepanyuk, 11 years

*My heart bleeds when I see wounded ATO (Anti
Terrorist Operation) heroes in the news, the
elderly crying, mothers who will never hear their
sons' voices.*

– Alexandra Konopatska, 16 years

– Volodymyr Yaschyk, 13 years

In Ukraine much evil has happened. For example, a war that destroyed thousands of Ukrainians.

The Great Famine, which nearly destroyed my country.

My soul becomes anxious whenever I recall what my native Ukraine has experienced and is experiencing, but I know that my nation is indestructible!

– Kateryna Hensetska, 14 years

I feel pain and sadness from the fact that war has come to Ukraine. I feel terrified for my future.
— Myroslava Kondratyuk, 9 years

I see in the future my country flourishing. My heart worries for the soldiers at war.
— Vadum Turkavsky, 9 years

Now there is war in East Ukraine. Soldiers die and many children became orphans.
— Valeriya Labai, 10 years

Every day soldiers die. I cry ... and pray for those in East Ukraine, who are defending our Motherland. I think, this will be all over, we have to believe it.
— Irma Kvartskhava, 10 years

I am very hurt by the fact that, East Ukraine is at war. I am very sorry for our wounded soldiers, the soldiers who died, but my heart is proud of them, our defenders. Every day I listen to the news and celebrate our every victory. I rejoice when people don't die.
— Denys Horban, 12 years

In the East there is a war that does not expire without leaving its marks. Every Ukrainian prays for peace in Ukraine.
— Kateryna Hensetska, 14 years

— Viktor Bodnar

Ukraine is experiencing difficult times: the Maidan, and stealing East Ukraine and Crimea.

Too many people have died.

These events really upset me even though I have a small heart.

— Ivanna Kulish, 9 years

Events, which are happening now in East Ukraine, make me very sad. A war comes, which takes the lives of adults and children. Evil and unmerciful people want to worsen another's grief. They stop and suppress our roots with their weeds and they don't allow peaceful growth. But I believe and know that Ukraine will win, because our heroes-soldiers aren't allowing blood to spread over all its regions.
— Andrij Kulish, 11 years

Because of those events, which are happening now in Ukraine, it is sad and painful, that so many people have died. My heart frets whenever I hear about these terrible events.
— Roman Kondratyuk, 12 years

Every day I pray for the soldiers of the ATO (Anti Terrorist Operation) and ask for peace.
— Vadum Nychyporuk, 13 years.

My heart feels the pain and horror because who would have thought, that our sister Russia would go to war on us.
— Diana Mikulska, 9 years

My heart feels pain for people, who suffer from the war in East Ukraine. Many teenagers have been left without homes.
— Valeria Labai, 10 years

I am bitter because of the war that is now happening in the East. After listening to stories about the Great World War, I never would have thought that all of this could happen in our time.
— Alina Lashchuk, 12 years

– Roman Veres, 4 years

Soldiers, who died on the front, are now in the sky. They didn't return to Earth.

– Valeriya Labai, 10 years

My heart aches about events, which are taking place in the East.
— Vadum Obidets, 12 years

In my opinion, this war is senseless and blood-thirsty. Young people go to war and many of them do not return. I always have questions: Why is it happening? How are our heroes going?
— Anna Vitriv, 13 years

Due to present events in the East, my heart feels sadness, pain for the dead.
— Serhiy Rabchuk, 14 years

I feel pain – soldiers and ordinary people are dying. War crushes a country.
– Valeriya Pyroh, 8 years

I believe that my mother Ukraine will bloom. And that my country will be free from invaders, but most importantly may our heroes return home with victory, healthy and happy.
– Anna Vitriv, 13 years

In the event that Ukraine will not overcome the enemy, we will need to accept the fate that falls upon our shoulders, that we will remain slaves in our own nation... forever.
– Sophia Yuzefko, 14 years

– Nadiya Lakoma, 14 years

Every Ukrainian asks for peace from God. Everybody wants to live freely and safely.

– Sophiya Yuzeffko, 14 years

War – this is terrifying, what can happen to the history of a country. People die in war, mostly those who didn't begin it. But when a terrorist comes to your home and intrudes on your freedom or territory. You must put him in his place. You must love your Motherland and protect her.
– Alexandra Feoktysova, 12 years

Let's remember those, who in winter,
In the final battle went to their death
We will not forget you – never!
Heroes don't lose – no-one!
If we knew how much more we must bear,
This suffering and torture of fire,
Surely we could not live,
From the grief and painful sorrow.
– Sophiya Yuzeffko, 14 years

My heart fills with blood, and my eyes fill with tears. I would like for the war to end quickly and for our heroes to come back to their beloved homes.
— Halyna Hurska, 17 years

It is very depressing, that there are misunderstandings between brotherly nations... This will not be!
We will become a wall of bricks for our country,
We will fight for peace and harmony.
We will break the political stranglehold
We believe in our country, we love her.
With Ukraine in our hearts we will live
With Ukraine in our hearts we will go to battle!
— Sophia Yuzvyk, 12 years

My heart aches, when I hear about the death of faithful Ukrainian soldiers. But every day I am glad, when we turn out raiders and Russian soldiers from our land.
– Anna Prysyazhna, 13 years

The biggest fear in the hearts of Ukrainians – is the war in the East of our country, where people die, for defending our unity and independence.
– Diana Moroz, 13 years

– Nadiya Lakoma, 14 years

I am bitter, because of what is happening in the East. I don't want them to destroy everything that has been created over the years. Let truth win in this war and let no more enemies step foot on our land!

– Valeriya Laschuk, 8 years

I worry and feel distressed because of events, which are happening in our country. I and my peers have witnessed the Revolution of Dignity, and now Eastern Ukraine is at war. My dad is also a member of the ATO (Anti Terrorist Operation). It is very difficult to wait for a dear person at war. You want time to pass very quickly and for the tears in mother's eyes to dry up. I dream of peace and tranquility in Ukraine.
– Daryna Stepanyuk, 12 years

I connect to those, whose heart cannot beat calmly, because they know, that their sons are dying. My heart will never live in peace, when it knows that something is threatening its country.
– Olga Kas'ko, 14 years

The word "war" is scary, sinister, chilling; it shakes every heart. And it all started with the Maidan. For each of us – this grief, loss, and wrongdoing is so painful, because it's about family, close friends, acquaintances. How many words have been said? How many tears have flowed, how many souls have fallen? And for what? For money? Power? We fight, pour out our blood, to obtain peace, calmness, freedom, our Ukrainian freedom and gratefulness for our patriotism, love for our dear land, respect for the memory of our ancestors, to the fallen at the Maidan, because we, like no one else, know the price of achieving freedom.
– Alina Muzychuk, 15 years

"America and Russia are to stay silent, when I speak with you" (V. Symonenko).
– Iryna Dubets, 15 years

War – is the worst, that can be. It is a huge loss, rivers of salty tears, and thoughtless decisions by the authorities. The war in our country is insane, it isn't even officially considered a war, it is called an anti-terrorist operation.
– Dariya Ripolovska, 14 years

Be blessed my Ukraine! They are tearing you to pieces, shooting, cutting, robbing.
– Daryna Stepanyuk, 12 years

The theme of the war for me is extremely painful. This is because innocent blood is shed, the blood of people who simply want to defend themselves and their country. Knowing about battles in the East, my heart bleeds.
– Natalia Hrebenyuk, 13 years

Thank you to our soldiers who defend us and the Ukrainian border from the enemy, we live in peace.
– Sophia Yuzeffko, 14 years

My heart is cut, whenever I remember, that they have always sought to conquer and capture Ukraine.
— Ulyana Kolesnik, 12 years

Drained, tired, broken
Fate is in shreds
Surrounded by misery and pain
The chords of melancholy music ring out.
In your eyes, huge tears brim
And your anguish has no measure
In your sky, lightning storms explode
They are saddened, that we live like this.
— Yuliya Petrushko, 15 years

*There is no Ukrainian, who would be indifferent
at a time, when his/her nation is being
destroyed. It hurts me that people are dying for
the independence and freedom of Ukraine.
However, the light will conquer darkness.
Glory to Ukraine!
Glory to our Heroes!*
– Serhii Tsekhosh, 12 years

*When everything in the East is being tortured
And they kill people in a moment
I can't sit idly, and not look at everything
And not think about it
While the authorities ignore us,
And our nation, and the war.
They just want the money.*
– Olga Kas'ko, 14 years

–Oleh Yaschyk, 11 years

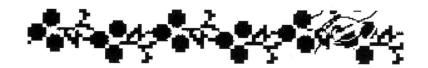

Ukraine is... a thick book with countless pages, and on the cover is the label "Warfare" written in human blood. The text is embroidered with red and black threads. It is a book that feels humanity's warmth and chill, love and hate. It is sprinkled with salty tears. It is completed with Ukrainian hearts.

– Iryna Dubets, 15 years

What can my heart feel, when injustice, corruption, and lies prosper everywhere? We – the children, don't want this. Students went to the Maidan, because they wanted to live in a European nation, and they killed them... What did the Nebesna Sotnya (Heavenly Hundreds) heroes die for? After all, nothing has changed.
– Olga Zhuk, 15 years

I really worry about Ukraine's fate. For those people, who died during the war and the Maidan. But I notice that Nebesna Sotnya (Heavenly Hundreds) died in vain.
– Yuriy Dyadyuk, 12 years

I love Ukraine for its patriotism, for its support, which it gave to the fighters, who are willing to give their lives for the sake of their people, for the sake of Ukraine – their homeland. Ukraine – is a small country, if compared with Russia, who wants to take our homeland. But Ukraine will not be handed over! She will go to battle to gain victory and overcome evil! Ukraine – I love you!
– Anastasiya Vasylyuk, 12 years

My heart is torn about the numerous deaths of soldiers, it is very agonising for me to watch the incomprehensible situation in the East. It's unpleasant to live with lies. But at the same time I am proud of our soldiers, they are real heroes!
– Sophiya Sal'nikova, 17 years

I feel pain and depression about events, which are taking place in the east of Ukraine, for he soldiers and their mothers. Why, in a time of high technology and the progress of humanity, do our brothers need to put guns in their hands for the defence of our land? Shame on our politicians, who rob and lie! People have forgotten their language and despise their own nation.
– Yuliya Loza, 12 years

About the war, which has happened in Ukraine, I feel the whole depth of this tragedy is not under anyone's power. Primarily, those Ukrainians who were killed in the Square, who died for honor, for freedom, for their homeland, have become our guardian Angels. They have been called the Heavenly Hundreds. They stood as examples of patriotism and love for this country.
Now it is our turn.
– Mariya Tsopko, 13 years

My heart is tearing apart... I cannot watch this calmly and indifferently. I always want to help in whatever way I can, the fighters in the ATO (Anti Terrorist Operation) zone, and people who live in the East.

– Diana Holdovans'ka, 13 years

In Ukraine now is a very difficult situation, because the invaders want to take our land. My heart is extremely anguished and worried. Do the politicians really want to continue this war, do they really not want Ukrainian soldiers to die? These questions really worry me. I want this war to end quickly.
– Solomiya Lukiyan, 13 years

My heart feels first of all – pain. I am just very sorry for the people, who fight for peace and honesty, and as a reward get – death.
– Yana Kurda, 14 years

Recently there was peace in the world, but a big mistake happened – because of it, a bloody war started. And when you look at the news and see with your own eyes, that so many innocent people are dying. This is a heavy stone on the soul, when you want to help but you can't, you're just a little kid. They tell you "Go to your room, and play", but you don't feel like it, when there is war in the world. Even though I am of no help at all, I believe in Ukraine! She will win! No war!
– Anastasiya Vasilyuk, 12 years

My heart only feels sorrow, despair, but I believe and pray, that God will stop this war, and soldiers will return home alive.
– Yuliya Shchebetyuk, 15 years

– Hakky Adanchuk, 6 years

Maidan... the heart of every Ukrainian remembers those terrible events, which took place there, at the Maidan... People were terrified, their hearts were chained to fear. The loudest gunshots rang out... One by one people fell to the ground. Many people died. And then, the Heavenly Hundreds, proudly spread their wings — soared into the sky, into the eternal memory of fallen heroes.

— Anna Kas'ko, 12 years

I thought that war – this was interesting history. Never would I have thought that in the 21st century the nation would witness such violence. Now I understand that war is the most terrifying crime against humanity. War deprives people of a roof over their head, work, life. The question: How do I feel about the war? There is only one answer, I am afraid!
– Inna Kurda, 16 years

Every time, I think of the soldiers, who died defending Ukraine, the fighters, who are out there, in the East, my heart aches and weeps.
– Anna Hayduk, 15 years

My heart aches from what is going on, especially in Eastern Ukraine. I feel sorry for those young men and boys, who died protecting us from enemies. How many children were orphaned because their parents died?
– Vadym Shtun 14 years

A terrible war has come to our land. Yes, we don't have an official announcement of war status. For some reason, they called all these terrible events in the East ATO (Anti Terrorist Operation). Every day, hundreds of brave, resilient soldiers die, that without a doubt went to rescue our Ukraine.
– Yulia Petrushko, 15 years

– Anastasiya Slota, 5 years

My heart aches, weeps and just rips apart from that, which is happening in Ukraine. An infinite number of young guys die, but their deaths bring no benefits to anyone, except hurt and suffering.

Russia has brought death to many homes. For what? What are they fighting for? A shred of land? Do they not have enough?

– Sofiya Davydyuk, 12 years

No one has the right to take away my yard and my bucket. Because they're my things! Who has the right to touch our land? Lands, that belong to my people. Lands, that keeps memories in them, that hold the blood of enemies and fellow countrymen in them. As yet, not one generation of Ukrainians has lived without war.

– Vladislav Bohun, 14 years

My heart breaks from the fact, that they killed students in Kyiv, knowing that all they wanted was a better life in their own native Ukraine. The Maidan's Heavenly Hundreds Square was already not hundreds, but thousands. Maidan ended but death continues...

– Mariya Krukovskaya, 13 years

We – are a strong nation. Our people are ready to fight for their land. The heart says – enough! And the the body is constantly bursting for battle.

– Iryna Dubets, 15 years

How do you see/want the future to be?

I Want Peace and Freedom...

СТОП ВІЙНІ!!

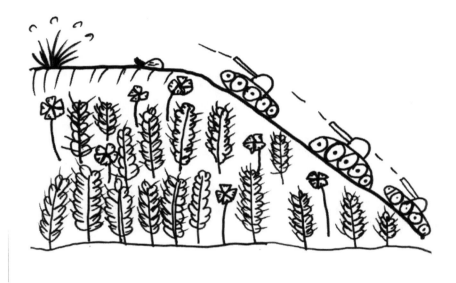

— Bohdan Zakhodnyak, 14 years

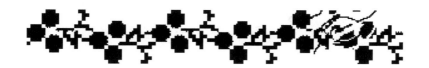

In the future my country is strong and rich, and other countries don't hurt her.

— Valeriya Peroh, 8 years

I see Ukraine as a rich, free, peaceful nation.
— Maxym Kamatska, 8 years

In a future I see my nation as being strong and independent. At school I diligently study the Ukrainian language.
— Alla Zvarko, 8 years

In the future I see my country free from Russian attackers. It will be a rich country, where good and honest people will live. They will take care of its development and peace. I believe that Ukraine will win and our heroes-soldiers will soon return home.
— Ivanna Kulish, 9 years

In the future I see my nation as free, independent and not destroyed. Now I see Ukraine with huge wounds. These wounds are called Luhansk region, Donetsk region and others.
– Yuliya Harbarchuk, 11 years

I am sure, that in the future my country will be free, peaceful, and rich. The army we have will be powerful and reliable.
– Mykhailo Rezhanovsky, 11 years

My nation in the future – this is a nation without war, without death, without Maidans. It will be a beautiful and wealthy country, where everyone always smiles and where everyone is always happy.
– Solomiya Lukiyan, 13 years

– Irynka Zakhodnyak, 14 years

Ukraine – I live in it
And I will die for it.

– Anna Prysyazna, 13 years

In the future Ukraine will be free. The houses, shops, and banks will be rebuilt in the East. For orphaned children parents will be found.
– Valeriya Labai, 10 years

I want, first of all a peaceful Ukraine, a Ukraine without war! I don't want anyone from Ukraine to go abroad in the hope of a better life. I want life to be better here, in Ukraine. Everyone must be a patriot of their country!
– Natalia Hrebenyuk, 13 years

I really love Ukraine and am happy that I was born here and live here. I love my Motherland and her beauty, and of course her immensely sincere and strong spirit, not only of Ukraine, but the Ukrainian people. Ukraine – is a peace-loving and powerful nation. I am sure that my country will win this difficult situation with Russia.
– Solomiya Lukiyan, 13 years

Ukraine – is strong. Ukraine – is independent. The Ukrainian nation has never and will never fall to its knees. We will win!
– Alla Zvarko, 8 years

I see my nation in the future as free and independent.
– Diana Mikulska, 9 years

Now for Ukraine is a hard time and every Ukrainian is concerned for his/her nation. I would like it if, our country lived in peace, without war.
— Yuliya Vavrenyuk, 14 years

Ukraine is a beautiful, rich, independent nation in which there are a lot of interesting beautiful places. People from other countries come to Ukraine, to admire her.
Whoever was born in Ukraine must be proud of his/her country. Because there is no such country in the whole world.
– Irma Kvartskhava, 10 years

– Irenka Zakhodnyak, 14 years

In these difficult situations, everyone needs to unite as a united whole, so that all other peoples see our will power and invincibility, to show, that Ukraine can also be independent, and not just a slave for others.

– Yulia Petrushko, 15 years

I see my nation in the future as happy and peaceful. Nobody will wage war, but only live in peace and prosperity. And also everyone will be friendly.
— Angelina Panasyuk, 10 years

In 1991 Ukraine became independent, but my heart shrinks in fear, of what is now happening in the east of Ukraine — this war. But I am sure, that the war will finish with Ukraine victorious. The best news is — the victory of the Crimean Jamala in the Eurovision competition. And so many people believe that the next competition will be held in Crimea.
— Yuliya Oshurkevych, 11 years

In a future there will be flying cars, more technologies and maybe even life on other planets. In the future, peace is waiting for us — peace in the world!
— Anastasia Vasylyuk, 12 years

In the future my country will be strong and rich, other countries will not exploit her.
– Valeriya Pyroh, 8 years

I wish for my people a peaceful and bright future. I want Ukraine to thrive and occupy a high place in society.
– Alina Lashchuk, 12 years

I dreamed of living in Japan, Greece, China, America... these wishes were as strong as I hated my fate, which identified Ukraine as my Motherland.
– Mykhailo Komatsky, 13 years

The future of our nation is in our hands. I think that in the future Ukraine will be an independent country, which will never be touched by war.
– Olga Kas'ko, 14 years

Ukraine's future is in our hands. In the hands of young people, who can change the life of our nation.
– Dariya Rìpolovs'ka, 14 years

In the future I see my nation free!
– Yuliya Vavrenyuk, 14 years

The hard-working and greatly distressed Ukrainian people deserve to live in a prosperous progressive country. In a nation where peace and fairness rule.
– Serhii Tsekhosh, 12 years

In the future I see my country as being powerful. Where everyone will speak pure, native Ukrainian, without mixed-Russian language. With the best education in the world.
– Anna Prysyazna, 13 years

Ukraine in the future – will be free and independent. This is a country that has endured many years of fighting for a place among strong nations, and, in my opinion, will survive this.
– Iryna Dubets, 15 years

My nation in the future — this is a nation without war, without death, without Maidans. But a beautiful and flourishing country, where everyone always smiles, where everyone is always happy.
— Solomiya Lukiyan, 13 years

I see... Ukraine has won the war. She triumphed over Russia. Now our Ukraine is free! Crimea is again ours!
— Diana Holdovans'ka, 13 years

I'm sure, that our country has a great future. A future without a past and present does not exist. I would like our fellow citizens to be kinder, better, so that they respect and love their native land, and the Motherland will answer them, and reciprocate.
— Yana Kurda, 14 years

I see my country as being free, democratic. I see Ukraine without war. I think, that in the future Ukraine will prosper, and we – her people, will be living no worse than other European countries.
– Halyna Hurska, 17 years

In the future, Ukrainian people will be happy and united. Ukraine will be a highly developed and prosperous nation in Europe, without corruption, without lies on the part of authorities.
– Sophiya Sal'nikova, 17 years

— Yuriya Slota, 7 years

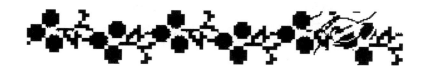

We will go to school in peace, gaining powerful knowledge. We will learn modern sciences and technologies. We will compare our minds in international competitions with children from other countries. We believe in the good glory of Ukraine, in the greatness of our people, in the growing power of our country in the future. We believe that Ukraine will become a full member of the European community. And we, the children, will live in harmony and happiness. May God help us with this! God, save Ukraine and her people!

– Diana Moroz, 13 years

I have dreamed for ten years to see our dear Ukraine as a financially secure nation. I dream for Ukraine to finally get up off her knees and proudly raise her head, delicately decorated with cornflowers.

I am sick and tired of watching Ukrainians from necessity, work in places for meagre wages, and have to travel for work to Poland, Russia and many other countries. This is humiliating for every one of us first and foremost for our Ukraine. Ukrainians, through their labour, develop foreign country, at a loss to their own.

Today let us now change native Ukraine, because every such change originally comes from the soul in each of us. Everything is in our hands. Let's move forward, to a bright future!

— Yuliya Petrushko, 15 years

In the future I see Ukraine without war. A united Ukraine! I sincerely believe, that this will be, enough of death from us.
– Mariya Krukovskaya, 13 years

Ukraine's future – this is a wonderful and a well-resourced nation. She is respected and valued in Europe. In the distant future I imagine my country as being strong and flourishing. Ukraine – is a strong country. I love and will always love her... I know – peace will come to the land
– Manuela Mindyuk, 13 years

I love you, oh land of mine,
That words cannot describe.
For you, native, dear,
I am ready to give up my life.

This is God's chosen land
Already it has beared so much.
So I believe that the time will come
For Ukraine to stand up.

She will rise from her knees,
And grow her wings.
And fly into a distant world
With her language, as nightingales sing.

– Yana Kurda, 14 years

My heart wants quiet and peace.
– Maxym Dudka, 8 years

I hope that my nation will become free and strong.
– Anna Kas'ko, 12 years

Of course, first of all, I want to see my country developed into a powerful state, which will manage different peoples in its own nation. I want to see realistic action aimed at keeping Ukraine safe.

– Vadym Shtun, 14 years

*I'm sure the day will come and war will end...
God does not judge us by our power, but judges
us by our actions. And those, who would deprive
us a piece of our soul – are bound to pay! But for
us – it will be a lesson. We will rebuild cities. And
we will go there with children, and cherish our
independence more.*

– Vladislava Bohun, 14 years

– Valentyk Shyshko, 11 years

Once upon a time on earth there lived a woman, who was called Ukraine, and her two sons were named – Ukrainians. They had a big house, which was overflowing with beautiful flowers from early spring until late autumn. The earth, which the mother and her children managed, was fertile and generous, which is why it was named Ukraine to honour the hard-working people. The sons grew strong and healthy. One of them wanted to go away to foreign lands, to see how people live. The mothers blessed the road ahead, even though her heart cried.

The son lived in a strange land for a long time, and when he returned, he was not alone, but with a wife and children. Although he grew up on this land and called himself Ukrainian, he forgot his mother tongue. His children spoke a foreign language also. But the mother's heart loved her sons, not wanting to come between them.

Their mother grew old and decided to pass the property for her children to inherit. The sons began to divide it but they couldn't reach an agreement. The heart of the mother cried, because even a scrap of bread she divided equally among them. The brothers took to battle and Ukraine overflowed with blood.

The ending this story depends on us – the grandchildren...

– Krystyna Morokh, 11 years

Thank You

Children in Ukraine would love to hear from you!

Many children in East Ukraine have lost their homes and families due to ongoing military attacks and aggressive terrorist activities. A prominent centre in Kyiv called *Dytynets* provides urgent care to extremely vulnerable children. Their charity program *Life Goes On* offers critical health and welfare services.

If you would like to say hello, learn more about the centre, or show support, please go to:

- www.facebook.com/pg/dytynets
- dytynets@gmail.com
- Telephone: +380970469889
- Fax: +380503829889

Made in the USA
Columbia, SC
18 March 2022

57815755R00076